Tie Dye Techniques

From Basics to Creative Patterns and Beyond

Copyright © 2023

All rights reserved.

DEDICATION

The author and publisher have provided this e-book to you for your personal use only. You may not make this e-book publicly available in any way. Copyright infringement is against the law. If you believe the copy of this e-book you are reading infringes on the author's copyright, please notify the publisher at: https://us.macmillan.com/piracy.

Contents

1. About Tie Dye   1

2. Tie Dye Supplies   4

3. How to Tie Dye: 6 Basic Steps   9

4. Tie-Dye Patterns and Folding Techniques   15

5. Tie Dying Other Items   44

6. Tie-Dye Shoes & Sneakers   46

7. Frequently Asked Questions   54

I. ABOUT TIE DYE

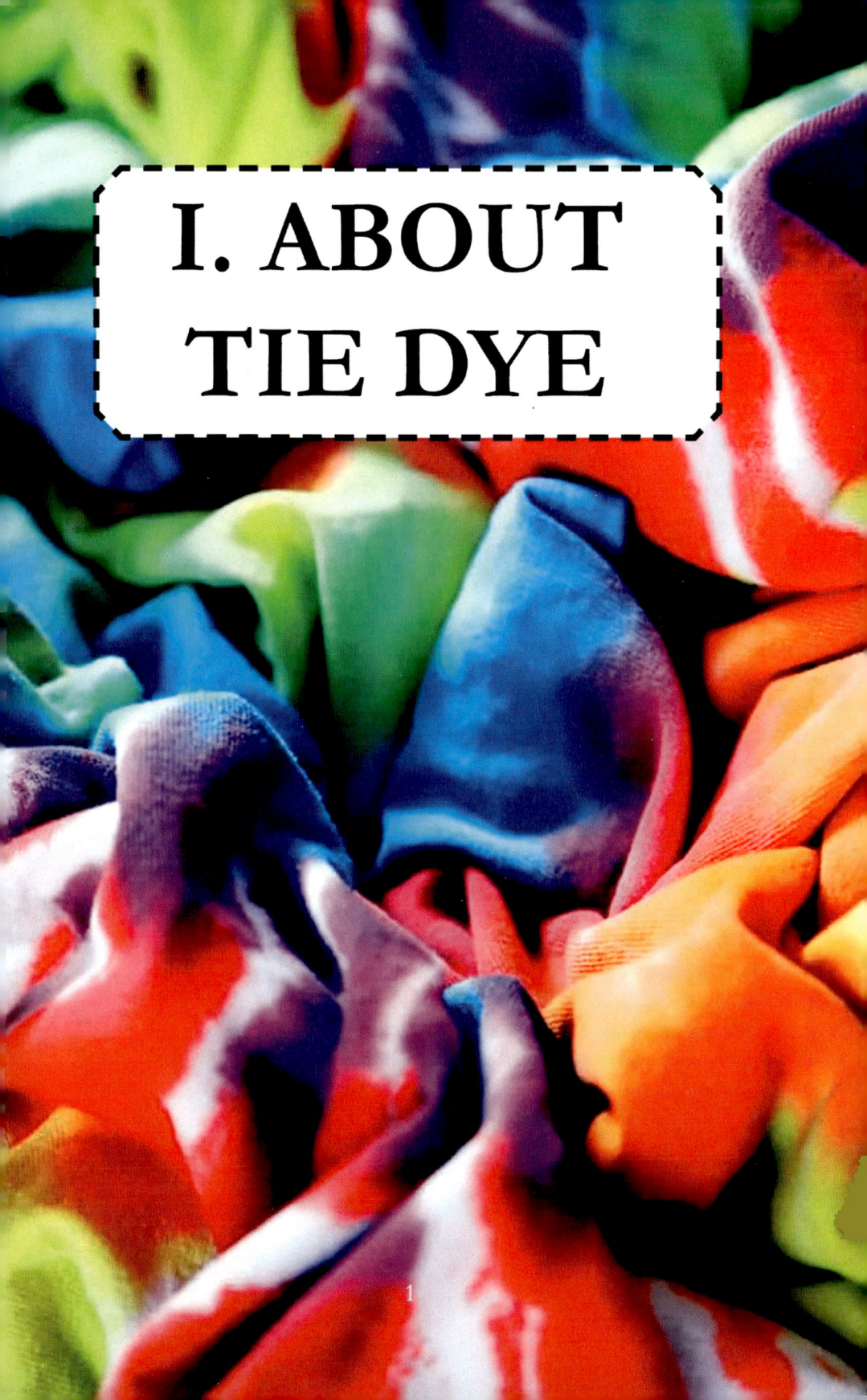

Tie-dye is a resist-dyeing technique that often uses bright, saturated colors and bold patterns. To tie dye, first, fold or crumple fabric and tie it with string or rubber bands. Then, dip the fabric in buckets of dye, or apply the dye with squirt bottles.

The folds and ties act as a resist, preventing the dye from saturating the fabric evenly. Any place that the dye can't reach will stay white, creating the design.

Types of Tie Dye

— Traditional Tie Dye —

The first is the most common type of tie-dye characterized by bright colors and bold patterns. This style was popularized in the 60s and 70s and remains trendy today. This type of tie-dye starts with a plain white shirt, which is then tied and dyed with one or more colors of liquid dye.

— Ice Dye —

Ice dying is similar to the traditional tie-dye, but the process is a little different. It starts the same, with a white or light-colored garment tied or secured with rubber bands. Then, the garment is covered in ice cubes and sprinkled with colors of powdered dye. As the ice melts, it will dissolve the dye powders and saturate the fabric. This type of tie dye can create some eye-catching organic designs.

— Tie Dye with Bleach —

Bleach tie dye, also called reverse tie dye, has become super popular in the last year or two. Bleach tie-dye starts with a black or dark-colored shirt, which is then tied and lightened with bleach. The bleach lightens the color of the exposed fabric, creating the tie-dye design.

II. TIE DYE SUPPLIES

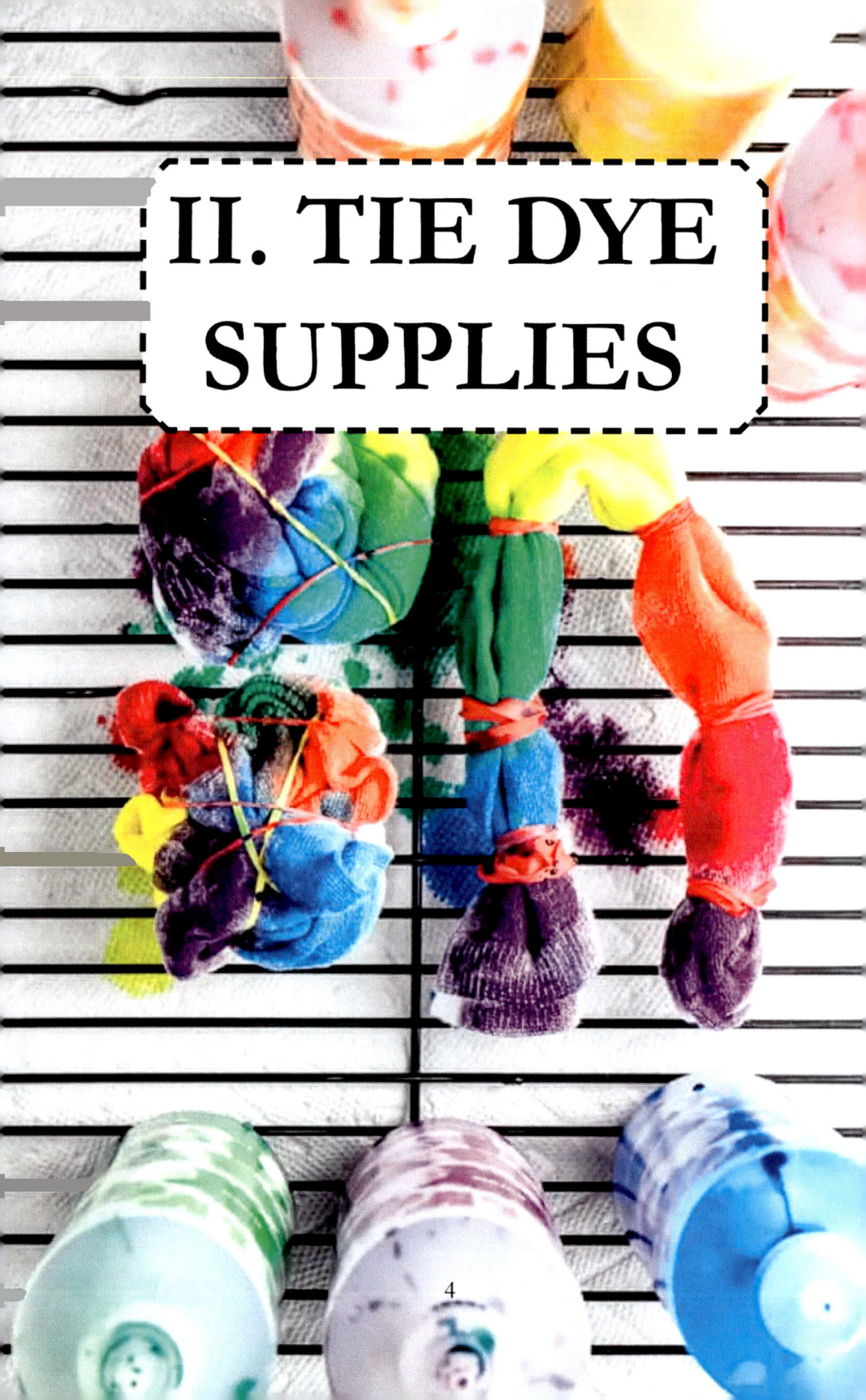

Before you can start dying, gather some supplies and materials. First and foremost, you'll need the dye itself and some fabric to dye. Then, you'll need to grab some tools and safety materials.

Here's what you'll need for this project.

- fiber-reactive dye in assorted colors
- fabric items, like shirts, socks, or sweatshirts
- soda ash (you may or may not need this, depending on the type of dye you purchase)
- Synthrapol, or another laundry detergent
- rubber bands or strong string
- buckets, to dip items in dye
- squeeze bottles, to apply dye
- plastic tablecloths or large trash bags to protect your work surface
- wire rack to elevate the garment off the work surface, *optional*
- gloves and a dust mask
- zip-top bags or plastic wrap

Best Dye for Tie Dying

The best type of dye to use on cotton fabrics for tie-dye projects is **fiber reactive dye**. This type of dye is much brighter, longer-lasting, and easier to use than other all-purpose dyes.

Fiber reactive dyes react with fabric in cold water to create a permanent bond – so you don't have to worry about your tie-dye design washing out the first time you put it in the laundry.

For this style of tie-dye, I **don't recommend using all-purpose dyes** like Rit or Dylon. In my experience, the colors are too pale and tend to wash out in hot water.

Types of Fiber Reactive Dye

Procion MX dyes: This is the most popular type of dye for tie-dye enthusiasts and professionals. Procion MX dye is colorfast, non-toxic, and very easy to use. Plus, it comes in a huge range of colors! You can find Procion dye kits from supplies like Jacquard or Dharma Trading Co.

Note: For best results, soak the shirt in a soda ash solution before dying with Procion dyes.

Tulip One-Step dyes: This type of dye is a great choice for the occasional tie-dyer, younger kids, and parties. The Tulip brand kits use a one-step dyeing process that eliminates the need to pre-soak fabrics in soda ash. The Tulip dyes are formulated with soda ash already in the dye powder, so all you have to do is add water, shake and apply.

Best Items to Tie Dye

You can dye all sorts of garments, like cotton shirts, sweatshirts, socks, even shoes! Items made with natural fibers are great for tie-dye. Look on the label for cotton, rayon, hemp, linen, or even silk.

Procion MX dye powders and the Tulip one-step kits are formulated to work with natural fibers, such as cotton, rayon, and silk. Synthetic materials such as polyester, nylon, Spandex, etc., do not absorb these dyes very well.

If you can't find 100% cotton shirts, you can use an 80/20 cotton/polyester blend, but the dye colors will not be as vibrant. Avoid 50/50 cotton/polyester blends because the dye will not react well, and the colors will come out very pale.

Here are a few cotton garments and items to tie-dye:

- women's shirts
- men's shirts
- kid's shirts
- hoodie
- socks (expect lighter colors due to fiber content)
- shoes/sneakers
- tote bags

III. HOW TO TIE DYE:
6 Basic Steps

In brief, here's how to tie dye.

1. Prep your supplies, and set up your work area.
2. Mix your dyes. Pre-soak your garment, if necessary.
3. Fold and tie your garment. (more on that below)
4. Apply the dye.
5. Let it sit. (The hardest part is waiting!)
6. Rinse, wash, and wear your garment.

Tie-dye is a pretty simple process, but there are a few tricks you need to know to get the best results.

Before we get started, let's go over a few safety tips.

- *Work outside or on a protected work surface.*
- *Be sure to wear old clothes or an apron.*
- *Wear gloves so the dye won't stain your hands.*
- *Wear a dust mask when mixing soda ash or dye powders.*

Alright, let's learn how to tie-dye.

Step 1. Prep the materials

Before you tie dye, you need to prewash the garments. Use a laundry detergent like Synthrapol to remove any oils, dirt, or anything else that might be on your garment. These things can resist the dye, leading to dull or spotty results.

Next, set up your work area. If you will dying inside, protect your table with a plastic tablecloth or large trash bags. It's a good idea to keep some paper towels or rags nearby to clean up any spills.

Then, gather your other tools, including plastic buckets, rubber bands, string, squeeze bottles, wire rack, and gloves.

Step 2. Mix your dyes. Pre-soak your garment, if necessary.

For Tulip One-Step dyes: all you need to do is add water to the dye bottles according to the package instructions and shake to mix.

For Procion MX dyes: Put on your dust mask and gloves. First, mix the dyes. Add 4 teaspoons of dye to a mixing bucket. Add a few teaspoons of lukewarm water to the dye powder – just enough to make a paste. Then, add 1 cup of lukewarm water to the bucket and stir to dissolve the dye. Ensure that you stir well and get rid of any lumps because the undissolved dye will leave spots of color or "freckles" on your finished garment.If you want, you can use a funnel to transfer the dye to squeeze bottles.

Then, make the soda ash solution. Add 1 cup of soda ash to 1 gallon of warm water. Stir to dissolve. Right before tie-dying, pre-soak your garments for 15 minutes. When time is up, squeeze out the excess solution so the fabric is damp but not dripping wet.

Step 3. Fold and tie your garment.

There are so many ways to fold and tie your fabric. Tie-dye techniques patterns range from simple to intricate. You can scrunch your garment, secure it with rubber bands, fold your garment, clamp it together, or even stitch a design into your garment with a needle and thread.

Step 4. Apply the dye.

There are many ways to apply the dye to the fabric. You can dip the garment into buckets of dye. Or, you can apply the dye directly to the fabric with squeeze bottles, paintbrushes, or sponges. You can use as many or as few colors as you want.

You can adjust the intensity of the colors by changing the dye-to-water ratio. If you want more pastel colors, you can add more water to the dye mixture.

When applying the dye, consider color placement. Think back to art class and the concept of the color wheel. Colors placed next to each other will bleed together at the border, creating new colors. Red placed next to yellow will create orange, green placed next to blue will create teal.

If you place complementary colors next to each other (that's red-green, orange-blue, or yellow-purple), you may create brown or other dull colors where the dyes bleed together.

Check out some of the tie-dye techniques down below to get some pattern inspiration!

Step 5. Let the dye set.

Once you have finished applying the dye, you need to give it time to react with the fabric. It's important to keep the fabric damp and relatively warm. (The warmer the temperature of the fabric, the quicker the dye reaction.)

I recommend placing the dyed fabric in a plastic bag or wrap it in plastic wrap. Place the wrapped fabric in a sunny spot, and let the dye process for at least 6-8 hours. For the brightest colors, you can let the dye cure for up to 24 hours.

Step 6. Rinse, wash, and wear your garment.

One of the keys to getting the cleanest, brightest colors is the washing-out process. Take your time here!

First, leaving the rubber bands or ties on, rinse the garment under cold running water. Then, continue rinsing in cool/lukewarm water while you remove the rubber bands or ties. Keep rinsing until the water runs clear. Then, run the garments through a complete warm/hot washing machine cycle with Synthrapol detergent.

For this first wash, you can wash multiple garments together, as long as they have been dyed with similar colors. If you wash too many colors together in the same load, the garments can come out muddy looking.

For the next couple of loads, you'll want to wash your tie-dyed clothing separately from the rest of your clothes. Then you can wash them with the rest of your colors.

IV. Tie-Dye Patterns and Folding Techniques

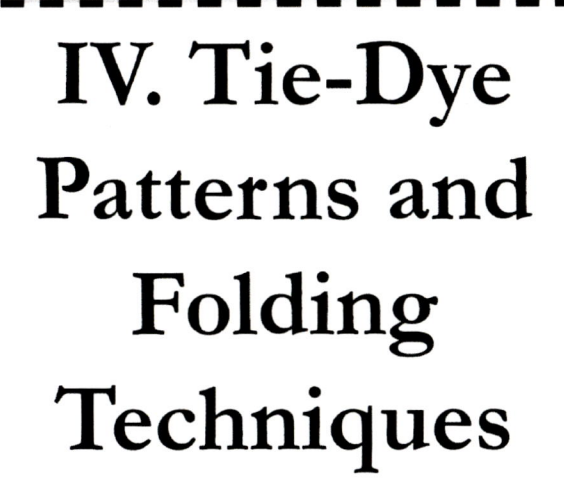

I'll teach you how to tie some of the most popular tie-dye patterns, such as the scrunch or crumple technique, the rainbow swirl pattern, shibori-inspired designs, and more. Here is a list of the tie-dye patterns we'll cover.

1. Spiral
2. Crumple
3. Bullseye
4. Sunburst
5. Horizontal Stripes
6. Vertical Stripes
7. Diagonal Stripes
8. Box Folds
9. Triangle Folds
10. Mandala aka Kaleidoscope
11. Heart
12. Rainbow
13. Chevron
14. Ombre Dip Dye
15. Socks – Stripes
16. Socks – Spiral
17. Socks – Crumple
18. Ice Dye (Bonus!)

1. Spiral or Swirl Tie Dye

To make a rainbow **spiral or swirl tie-dye shirt:**

1. Start by pinching a small section in the center of the shirt. Hold on to that small section while you twist the shirt clockwise.

2. Keep twisting, keeping your fingers close to the surface of the table so the spiral stays flat

3. As you twist, the shirt will fold in on itself like a flat cinnamon roll.

4. Secure the shirt with 3 or 4 rubber bands, crisscrossing them over the center of the disc. The tighter you bind the shirt, the more white areas there will be.

5. Apply a different color of dye in each "wedge" created by the crisscrossing rubber bands. Apply the dye in rainbow order to get a rainbow spiral design.

2. Scrunch or Crumple Tie Dye

To make a **crumple tie dye aka "scrunch" design:**

1. First, lay the shirt flat. Then, scrunch smaller sections of the fabric together randomly.

2. Keep scrunching and folding, gathering all of the fabric into a relatively flat, tight disk.

3. Wrap several rubber bands around the disk. The tighter you scrunch it, the more white areas there will be in the final shirt.

3. Bullseye Tie Dye Pattern

To make a **large bullseye design:**

1. Lay the shirt flat on a table. Pinch a small section of fabric at the center of the shirt. (If you want the bullseye to be off-center, choose a small section off-center.)

2. Pull the pinched fabric up to a point, and smooth the rest of the shirt down to create a skinny cone shape.

3. Wrap rubber bands around the cone of fabric, starting about an inch below the point of the cone. You can add as many or as few rubber bands as you want.

4. To make stripes, apply alternating colors of dye.

4. Sunburst Design

23

The sunburst design is like a series of small bullseyes. To make the **sunburst tie-dye pattern:**

1. Lay the shirt flat on a table. Pinch a small section of fabric, and pull it up to create a small pointed cone shape.

2. Wrap a rubber band around the small cone of fabric, about 1/2 to 1 inch down from the point of the cone.

3. Repeat this process, pinching another small section of fabric to create another cone. Secure with a rubber band.

4. Make as many sunbursts as you like.

5. Apply 1 or 2 colors of dye for the background color.

5. Horizontal Stripes

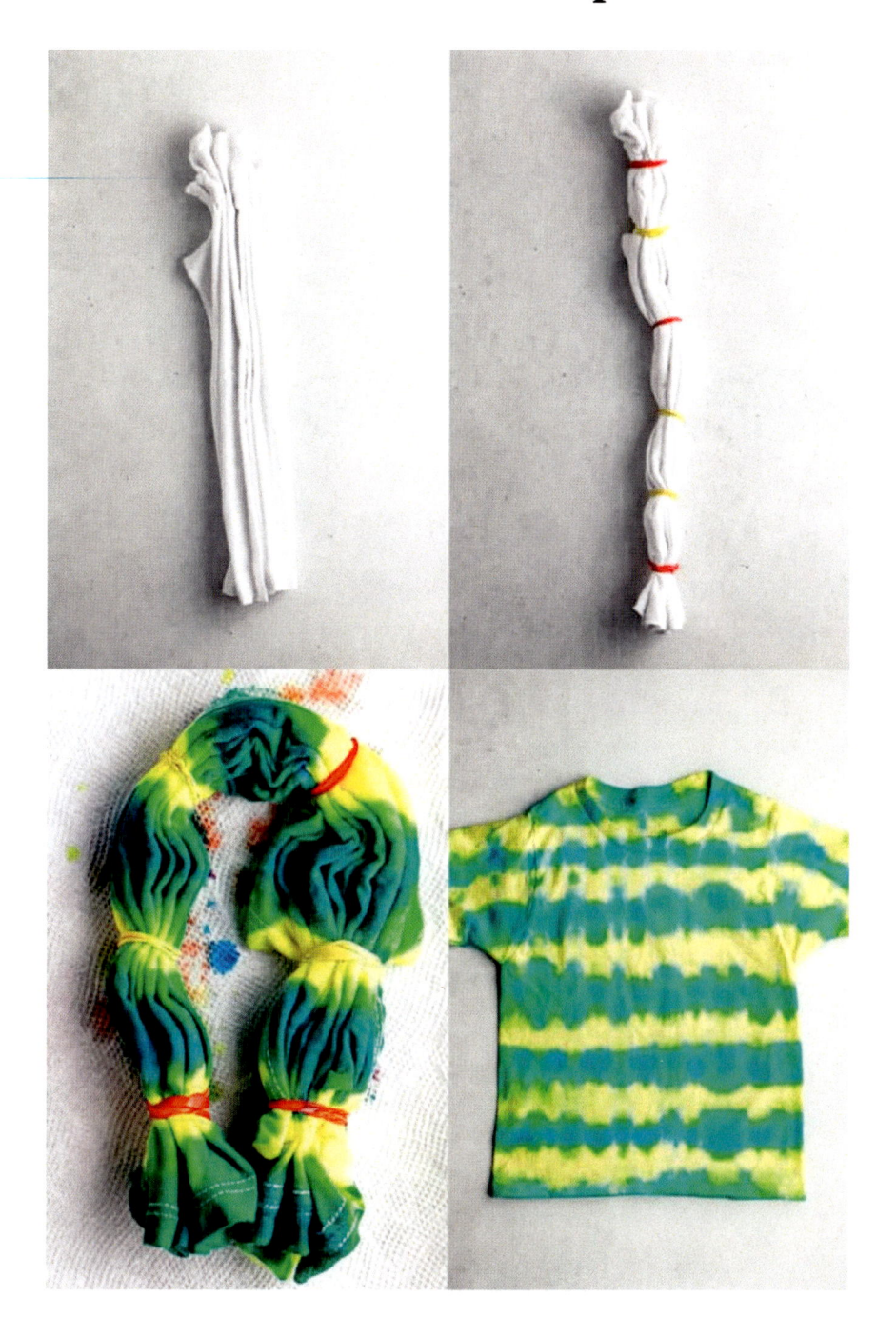

To make **horizontal stripes:**

1. Lay the shirt flat. Starting from the left sleeve, fold the shirt in a series of 1" accordion folds. Alternate the folds back and forth, like you're making a paper fan.

2. Secure the folded shirt with rubber bands, placing a rubber band every 1 to 2 inches.

3. To create stripes, apply dye colors in alternating sections.

6. Vertical Stripes

Making vertical stripes is very similar to making horizontal stripes. To make **vertical stripes:**

1. Lay the shirt flat. Starting from the bottom hem, fold the shirt in a series of 1" accordion folds. Alternate the folds back and forth, like you're making a paper fan.

2. Secure the folded shirt with rubber bands, placing a rubber band every 1 to 2 inches.

3. To create stripes, apply dye colors in alternating sections.

7. Diagonal Stripes

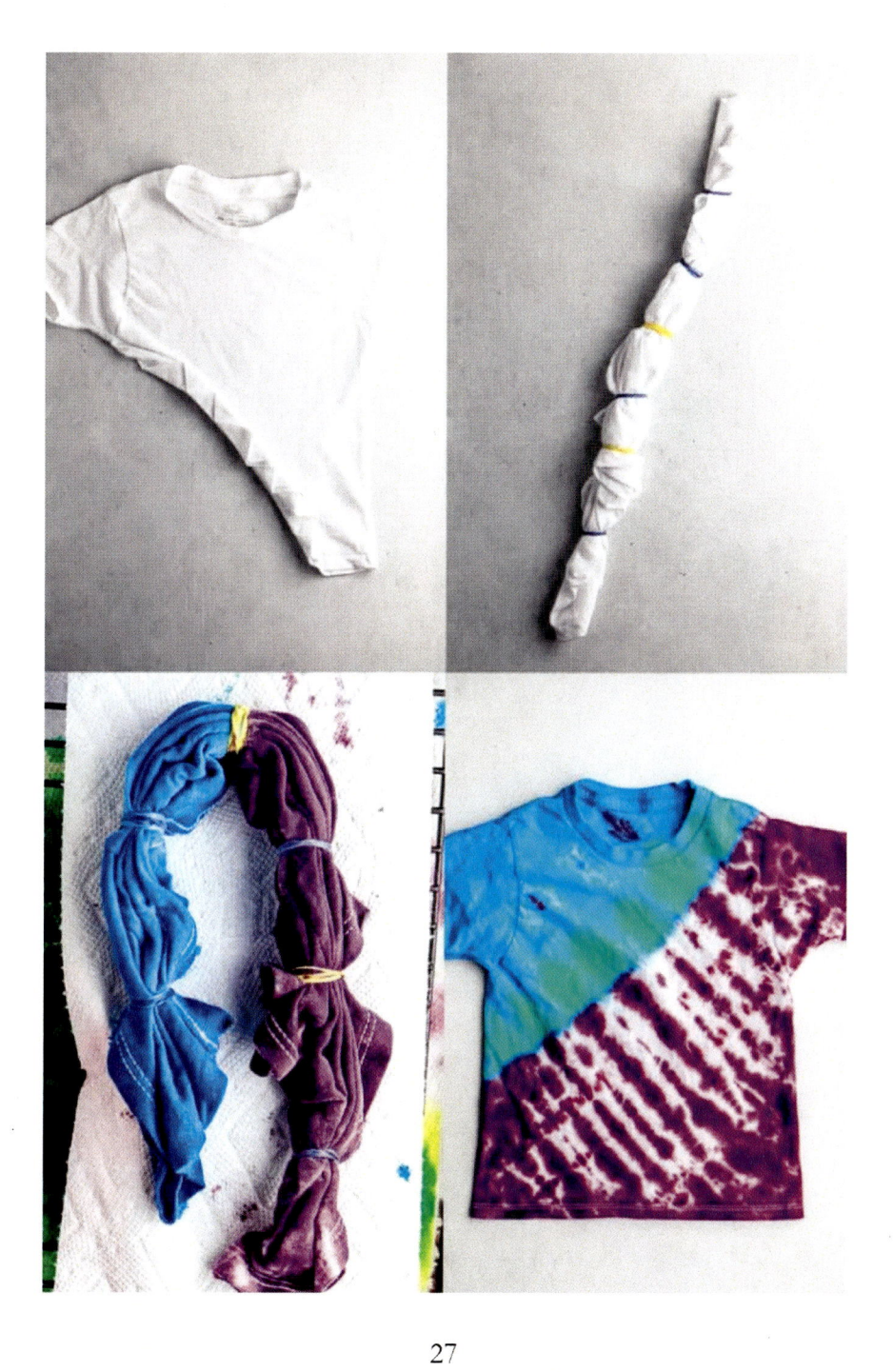

To make **diagonal stripes:**

1. Lay the shirt flat. Starting from the bottom-left corner, fold the shirt in a series of 1" accordion folds. Alternate the folds back and forth, like you're making a paper fan.

2. Folding the left sleeve can be a little tricky, but try to keep it in line with the rest of the folds.

3. Secure the folded shirt with rubber bands, placing a rubber band every 1 to 2 inches.

4. To create stripes, apply dye colors in alternating sections. Or, create a color-blocked design like the shirt in the pictures above.

8. Square Box Folds

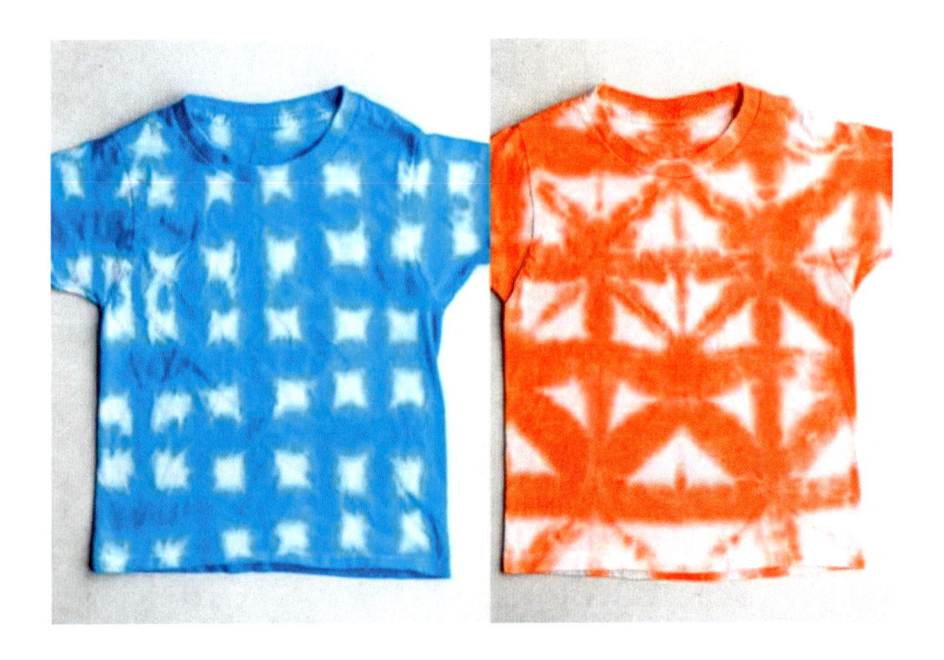

In the pictures above, reference the diagram on the left and the finished blue shirt. To make **shibori-inspired square folds:**

1. Lay the shirt flat on the table. Starting on the left side, fold the shirt lengthwise in a series of accordion folds. I made each fold about 3.5 inches wide. Press the edges of each fold well to get sharp creases.

2. Next, fold the shirt widthwise in a series of accordion folds. I made each fold about 3.5 inches wide to match. The resulting bundle of fabric should be a square shape.

3. Sandwich the fabric bundle between two 3" squares of cardboard. Secure well with rubber bands.

4. You can dip the bundle in a bucket of dye, or use a squeeze bottle to apply dye to the edges of the bundle.

9. Triangle Folds

This technique starts out the same way as the previous design. In the pictures above, reference the folding diagram on the right and the finished orange shirt. To make **shibori-inspired triangle folds:**

1. Lay the shirt flat on the table. Starting on the left side, fold the shirt lengthwise in a series of accordion folds. I made each fold about 5 inches wide. Press the edges of each fold well to get sharp creases.

2. Next, fold the shirt up into triangles. If you've ever folded a flag, this will be familiar. Fold forward up, then back over at a 45-degree angle. Fold forward up again, then back over at a 45-degree again. Repeat until all of the fabric is folded. The resulting bundle of fabric should be a triangle shape.

3. Sandwich the fabric bundle between two matching triangles of cardboard. Secure well with rubber bands.

4. You can dip the bundle in a bucket of dye, or use a squeeze bottle to apply dye to the edges of the bundle.

10. Mandala aka Kaleidoscope Tie Dye

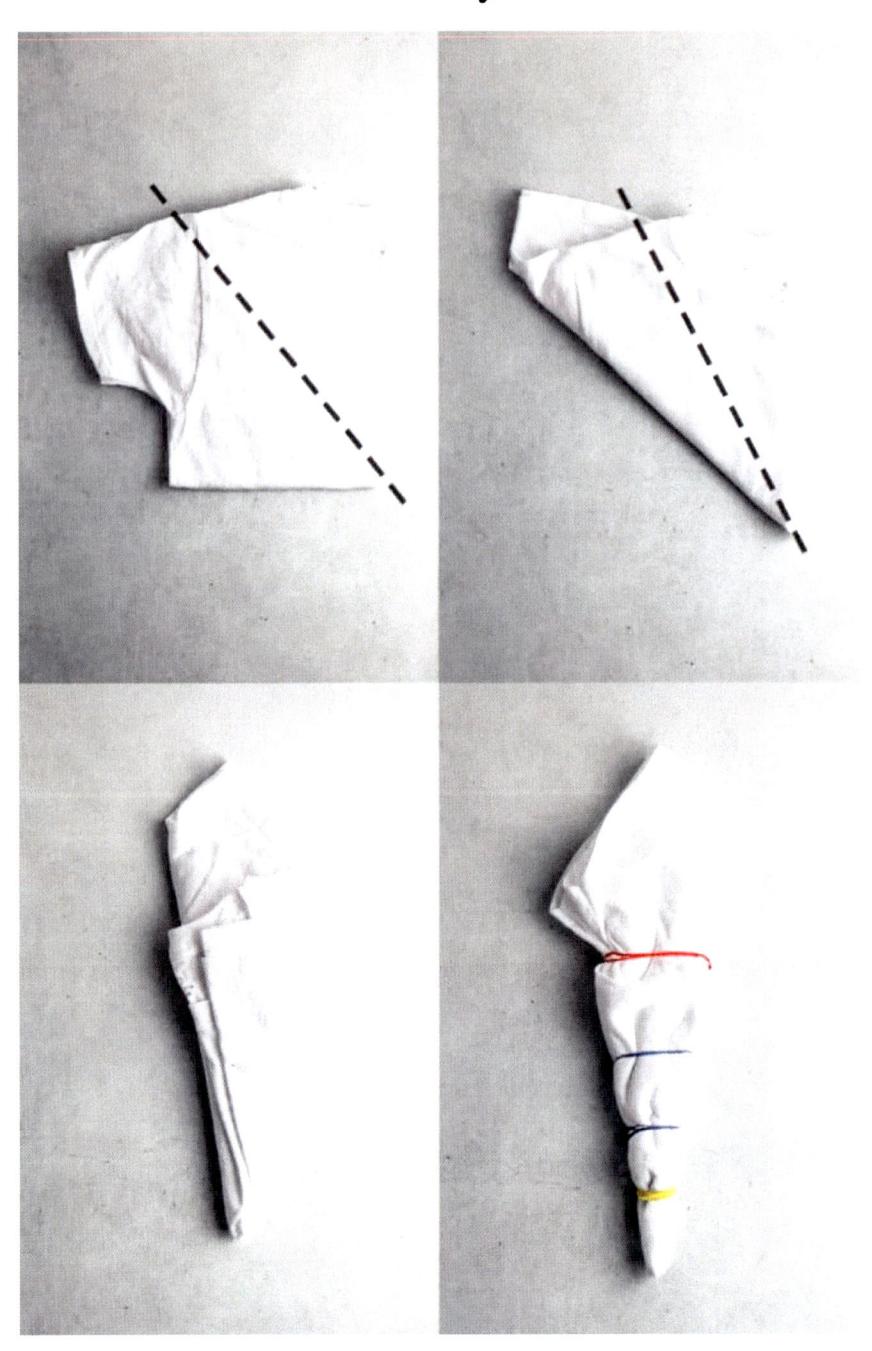

For this look, you'll be creating a design with multiple lines of symmetry. To make a **tie-dye mandala design:**

1. Lay the shirt out on the table. Fold it in half lengthwise. Then fold in half again widthwise. The shirt is now folded into quarters.

2. Following the diagram above, fold the shirt in half along the diagonal line. The shirt is now folded in eighths.

3. Following the diagram above, fold the shirt in half again along the diagonal line. The shirt is now folded into sixteenths.

4. Secure with rubber bands.

5. Apply the dye in various colors to create your unique design.

11. Heart Tie Dye

With a little patience, you can fold the fabric to create a tie-dye heart in the middle of the shirt. Here's how to make a **tie-dye heart:**

1. First, lay the shirt out flat. Then, fold the shirt in half lengthwise.

2. Draw half of a heart shape on the folded edge with a washable marker.

3. Starting at one end of your line, begin making small accordion pleats. Follow along the drawn line, folding the pleats in such as way that the marker line appears straight on the top of the folds. This means that you'll be making the pleats a little deeper on the outside section and a little shallower on the inside section to accommodate the curve of the line.

4. When all of the fabric has been pleated, secure it with a thick rubber band. Put a runner band on the line itself, and add more rubber bands on the inside or outside sections as desired.

12. Rainbow Tie Dye

Here's how to make a tie-dye **rainbow shape:**

1. First, lay the shirt out flat. Then, fold the shirt in half lengthwise.

2. Draw half of a rainbow arch on the folded edge with a washable marker.

3. Starting at one end of your line, begin making small accordion pleats. Follow along the drawn line, folding the pleats in such as way that the marker line appears straight on the top of the folds. This means that you'll be making the pleats a little deeper on the outside section and a little shallower on the inside section to accommodate the curve of the line.

4. When all of the fabric has been pleated, secure it with a thick rubber band. Put a runner band on the line itself, and add more rubber bands on the inside or outside sections as desired.

5. Apply the dye in rainbow order to create a traditional rainbow color scheme.

13. Chevron Tie Dye

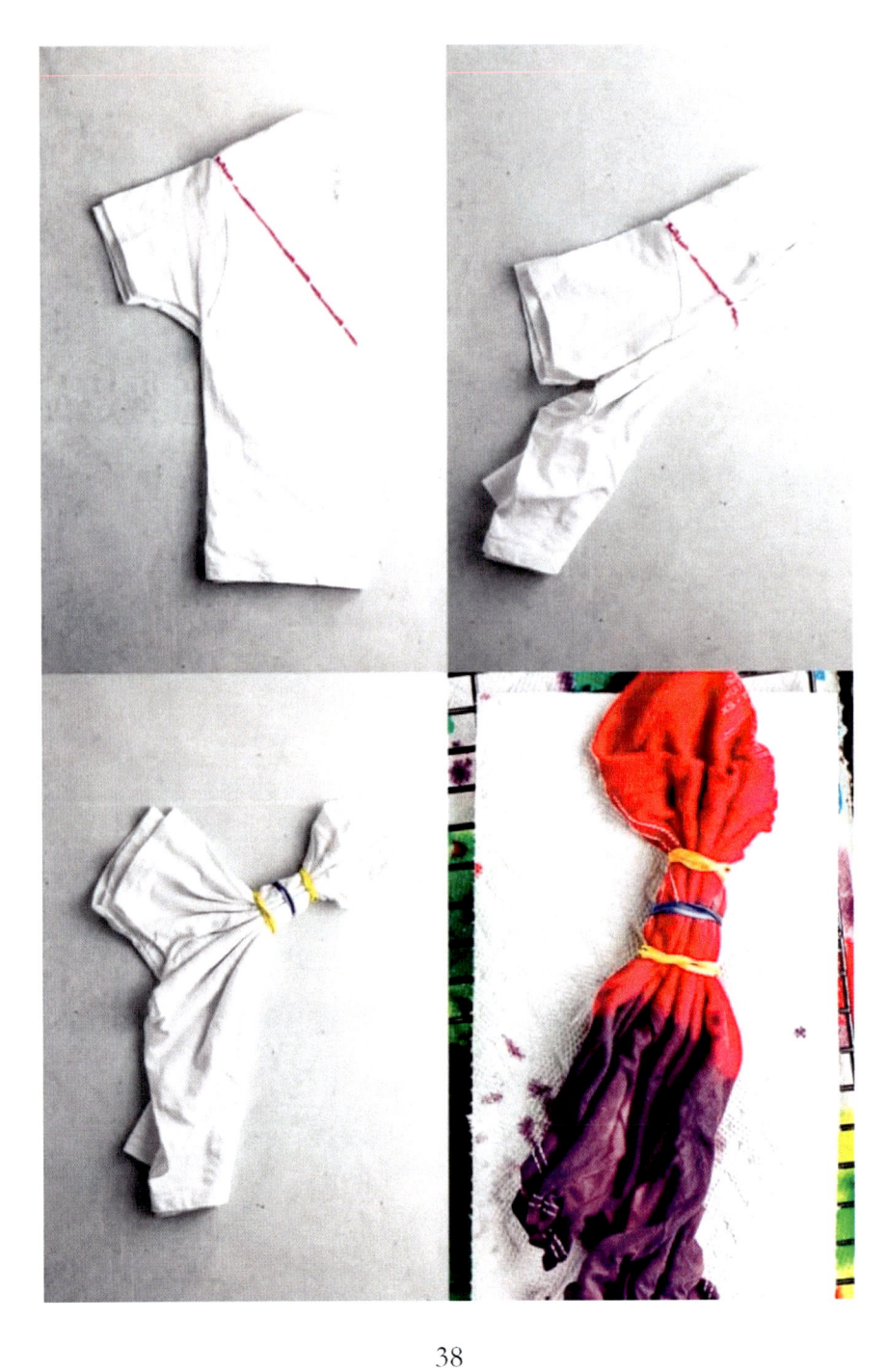

This chevron design is a variation of the diagonal stripe designs that we learned above. Here's how to make a **tie-dye chevron:**

1. First, lay the shirt out flat. Then, fold the shirt in half lengthwise.

2. Draw half of a chevron V-shape on the folded edge with a washable marker. You can position it higher or lower than mine, or make it pointing upward or downward – your choice.

3. Starting at one end of your line, begin making small accordion pleats. Follow along the drawn line, folding the pleats in such as way that the marker line appears straight on the top of the folds.

4. When all of the fabric has been pleated, secure it with a thick rubber band. Put a runner band on the line itself, and add more rubber bands on the inside or outside sections as desired.

5. For a color-blocked look, add 1 or two colors of dye. For a striped chevron look, apply dye in small sections, alternating colors.

14. Ombre Dip Dye

For this technique, you don't have to fold the fabric – though I think it would look really awesome with some thin accordion folds! To make an **ombre dip dye design:**

1. Dip one end of the shirt into a bucket of dye. As it sits in the dye bath, the dye will slowly work its way up the fabric.

2. You can repeat this process by dipping the other end of the fabric into a different color of dye.

15. Striped Tie Dye Socks

Tie-dying socks is very similar to shirts – you just have a smaller canvas to work with. To create a pair of matching **tie-dye striped socks:**

1. Lay two socks together, and fold them in half lengthwise.

2. Place a rubber band every inch or two down the length of the socks.

3. Apply a different color of dye in each section.

17. Crumple Dye Socks

Here's the easier way to dye socks. You can dye them as a pair, or as singles. To make **crumple dye socks:**

1. First, lay the socks flat. Then, scrunch small sections of the fabric together randomly.

2. Keep scrunching and folding, gathering the socks into a relatively flat, tight disk.

3. Wrap several rubber bands around the disk. Apply the dye in the colors of your choice.

16. Swirl Dye Socks

Since socks don't have lot of surface area, it's hard to get a true spiral. Even so, I really like the design that this technique makes. To make **swirl tie dye socks:**

1. Lay two socks together. Pinch a small section in the heel area, and twist. Keep twisting until the socks coil up on themselves, like a cinnamon roll.

3. Secure with rubber bands. Add different colors of dye to the "wedges" that are formed by the crisscrossing rubber bands.

Bonus: Ice Dye

Ice dying is a fun and cool variation on traditional tie-dying techniques. I love it for the way it creates stunning watercolor designs. Instead of liquid dye and squeeze bottles, ice tie dye uses powdered dye sprinkled over a pile of ice cubes.

V. TIE DYING OTHER ITEMS

Don't stop at shirts! There are all sorts of other garments and items you can tie-dye: hoodies, sweatpants, headbands, socks, and even sneakers. When you're shopping, look for garments with a very high percentage of cotton or other natural fiber.

How to Dye Hoodies and Sweatpants

Thicker fabrics like sweatshirts and sweatpants work really well with more organic techniques, like the crumple technique, the swirl pattern, and stripes. While you can do the more intricate designs on thicker materials, it may be a little tricker.

How to Tie Dye Sneakers

You can even dye cotton canvas sneakers. Remove the laces and liners before you start, and soak them upside down in warm water and a little bit of Synthrapol to "prewash" them.

You can't actually scrunch them up and tie them with rubber bands, but you can dip them in buckets of dye or apply the dye with squirt bottles, paintbrushes, or sponges.

How to Tie Dye Socks

Socks are easy and fun to tie-dye. If you want matching socks, you can tie them up together and dye them at the same time. Since they have a small surface area, you can't make large mandala patterns, though.

VI. TIE-DYE SHOES & SNEAKERS

Learn how to tie dye shoes and enjoy wearing unique shoes all year round. Get inspired with different styles of tie dye shoes for men and women— there are endless ways to tie dye and customize your casual canvas shoes, spiffy sneaker shoes, everyday running shoes and more! Read on to find different tie-dye designs to try and get inspired to create your own colorful kicks with Tulip!

What you need:

Tulip One-Step Tie Dye Kit

Natural fiber fabric shoes

Wire rack + baking sheet or protective surface cover

Masking tape

Optional Materials:

Disposable shallow tray

Disposable cups

Embellishments

Shaving cream

Paintbrush

Ice

How to marble tie dye shoes with shaving cream

1. Tape

Before you tie dye shoes, use masking tape to block off any areas you don't want dyed. This method works best with slip-on canvas shoes because of the flat surface area, but you can try it with any natural fiber fabric shoes!

2. Marble

Cover your work area with a protective surface cover. Add shaving cream to a shallow pan and drizzle your desired color(s) of dye to the top. Use a spatula to swirl and create a marbled pattern.

3. Dip

Carefully dip each shoe into the marbled shaving cream.

4. Scrape

Scrape off excess shaving cream with the spatula and use a paper towel to clean off any additional product. Let dry for the dye to completely set, then remove tape.

5. Reveal!

These swirled shoes look super! The Tulip Marbling 4-Color Tie-Dye Kit has almost everything you need to try this technique— just add shaving cream!

How to ombré tie dye shoes

1. Tape

Before you tie dye shoes, use masking tape to block off any areas you don't want dyed. The ombré tie dye method works on any natural fiber fabric shoes, such as slip-on canvas shoes, sneaker shoes, and running shoes!

2. Pour

Pour One-Step Tie-Dye into cups for ease of use and place your shoes onto a protected work surface.

3. Brush

Use a paintbrush to apply dye to the shoes. Dip paintbrush in water and brush dye upwards to create a gradation of the original color and blend into the next. Let dry for the dye to completely set, then remove tape.

4. Embellish

Embellishments are optional but are great for adding a touch of personalization to your tie-dyed shoes!

5. Reveal!

Aren't these ombré tie-dye shoes adorable? Try this technique with any of your favorite Tulip One-Step Tie-Dye Kits and easily create awesome ombré designs!

51

How to ice tie dye shoes

1. Tape

Before you tie dye shoes, remove the laces and use masking tape to block off any areas you don't want dyed. The ice dye technique works on any natural fiber fabric shoes, such as slip-on canvas shoes, sneaker shoes, and running shoes!

2. Ice

Place shoes onto a wire rack over a baking sheet or plastic bin. Pile ice over the shoes, making sure you cover as much of the shoes as possible with ice. The tray will collect the runoff from ice and dyes as the ice melts.

3. Dye

Sprinkle the dry dye powder(s) over the top of the ice. As the ice melts overnight, it'll transfer the dyes to the shoes! Let dry for the dye to completely set, then remove tape.

4. Reveal!

Your tie-dye shoes are ready to wear! Try this technique with the Tulip One-Step Ice Dye Kit for super cool tie-dye effects.

VII. Frequently Asked Questions

Do you need to prewash the fabric before dyeing it?

Yes. Prewash your garments in detergent, such as Synthrapol, before dying. Prewashing removes dirt, oils, and sizing that can prevent the dye from penetrating the fabric.

Do you tie-dye wet or dry fabric?

In most cases, I recommend tie-dyeing fabric that is slightly damp but not dripping wet. When the garment is wet, the dye will more easily saturate the material, leading to more even coverage. That said, you are welcome to experiment with applying dye to dry fabric. Applying dye to dry fabric will result in less uniform saturation and more white spots.

How long should tie-dye set before rinsing?

It's important to set the tie dye for several hours to get the brightest colors possible. After dying, wrap your garment in plastic (or place it in a zip-top bag) and let it sit for at least 6-8 hours. This processing time helps the dye soak into the fibers of the fabric. If you have more time, you can let the dye sit overnight or up to 24 hours.

How do you wash tie-dye shirts for the first time?

Before washing your tie-dyed garments in the washing machine, rinse them under running water until the water runs clear. Put the newly tie-dyed fabric into the washing machine by itself and run it through a cold water/delicate cycle with Synthrapol or another color-safe detergent.

To be extra safe, wash your tie-dyed garments separately for a few washes before washing them with the rest of your laundry.

How do you make tie-dye colors brighter?

The best way to get bright tie-dye colors is to use the right kind of fiber-reactive dye and 100% cotton fabric. Then, remember to prewash your fabric and soak it in a soda ash solution (if your dye requires it.) Be patient and let the dye cure for up to 24 hours for the best color saturation. Click this link to learn more about how to set tie dye so it doesn't fade.

Can you set dye in the microwave?

If you can't wait the full 24 hours before rinsing out your newly dyed items, you can try speeding up the process with a microwave oven.

Heating the garments in a microwave accelerates the dye reaction so that you can wash them out after a few minutes rather than several hours.

Note: Be careful, and only attempt this under adult supervision. Microwave in small time increments, and use your best judgment.

To process tie-dye in the microwave:

1. Place the garment into a heavy-duty gallon-size zip-lock freezer bag, and squeeze out all the air.

2. Seal the bag and microwave it for 60-90 seconds.

3. Watch the bag closely, and stop the microwave when the bag inflates with steam – you don't want the bag to pop!

4. The goal is to heat the garment all the way through, but not heat it so much that any part of it dries out. The actual time required to heat the garment will vary.

Let the garment cool, and then rinse it out as directed above.

Made in United States
Orlando, FL
19 June 2025